pieces of christmas

pieces of christmas

by RUTH ESTELYN HILLMAN

THE BETHANY PRESS
SAINT LOUIS   MISSOURI

© 1975 by The Bethany Press

All rights reserved. No part of this book may be reproduced by any method without the publisher's written permission. Address The Bethany Press Box 179, St. Louis, Mo. 63166

Library of Congress Cataloging in Publication Data

Hillman, Ruth Estelyn, 1925-

   Pieces of Christmas

   1. Christmas—United States. I. Title.
GT4986.A1H55   394.2'68282   75-19362
ISBN 0-8272-2923-2

Cover art by Dorothy J. Eicks

Manufactured in the United States of America

For my husband

FOREWORD

Christmas is such an overwhelming time that its many complex parts seem to stand importantly alone. Each person has his storehouse of Christmas memories—each has specific, once-in-a-lifetime happenings which hang and dangle through time and glitter brighter as Christmas draws nearer. Yet Christmas is more than incidents strung together with tinseled time. Christmas is a loving time, a giving time, and, strangely, a hurting time.

Christmas is a sensitive season of deep depression for some people. My feelings at Christmas, no matter how gala the occasion, are based on an aura pensive, anxious, and sad. Why? I've never understood. Maybe it's a little like the feeling Emily Dickinson felt when she wrote, "I dreaded that first robin so." Perhaps the intense beauty, the sweet dearness of robins and Christmases, and all the things man knows and cannot keep, cause a deep wave of sadness underneath the spurts of joy.

This little book, started on a cold December evening a week before Christmas, will be my attempt to gather together my pieces of Christmas. They won't fit together like jigsaw-puzzle parts, I'm sure. Yet, I need to look at the pieces, some jagged and dangerous, some safe and sensible, and attempt to meld them into a Christmas whole. And when they are pressed together in book pages, perhaps the sharp edges will dull with comfortable tradition and pieces of Christmas will become like hard candy—bright and sweet to my taste.

Contents

Churches 11

Homes 21

Returning 31

Innocents 39

Songs 47

Traditions 57

Morning 67

Angels 75

Still 83

churches

Christmas time at church. The rehearsals, the plans, the chaos, the excitement. When I think of events pertaining to Christmas, I naturally center some of the most festive ones in the church—the result of Christmas in the first place.

A kaleidoscope of Christmas-church pictures turns in my mind. Where shall I stop to focus on clarity? Shall I arrange the pictures chronologically or first come, first served? Perhaps the glimpses shall categorize themselves into a meaningful panorama. Although organization is a prerequisite for any worthwhile writing, I choose to be bold and defy custom and let my bright pieces of Christmas fall and shine where they may.

The scene is the tall church on North Walnut Street. The time: the annual Christmas program. Up in front on the platform, before a packed audience, stands my second son. He is blond and lively and went up front, nearly strutting, when his name was called. He turned, bold as brass, faced the huge group of smiling people, and ZONK! He was scared to death!

There he stood in his four-year-old fright looking like a big doll with his hair parted and comb marks neatening up his head like rays.

And there I sat, nearly bursting with pride as I watched him strut on stage. Then fear filled my mouth with chalk dust as I saw his stage fright freeze him.

"How does it start, Mommy?" he managed to squeak, looking into the sea of faces for me. Although I had drilled him since Thanksgiving, I couldn't think of a thing.

The program director, bless her forgotten name, gave him the first line and he said his "piece" not once, but three times.

> "Jesus, blessed Jesus,
> Little Lord divine,
> Oh, how we adore Thee,
> Dear Babe of Christmas time."

He bowed low and left the platform with dignity as murmurs of adoration filled the huge room.

The next piece of Christmas-church picture I want to focus on happened in little Bethlehem Church. On the platform this unseasonably warm Sunday before Christmas, were several children, including three shepherds. One of them was my first son, aged ten. He wore an old blue-fringed woolen head scarf draped low over his forehead, and a heavy plaid bathrobe over his Sunday suit. He carried a cane pole.

His dull-eyed expression vexed me, because I thought he was bored. All of the shepherds were similarly attired, so his costume was nothing out of the ordinary.

I sat about halfway back trying to keep my three-year-old son quiet. He recognized his brother up front in the strange garb and seemed determined to get his attention.

Mary and Joseph were uttering their dialogue and gesturing over a doll in a straw-filled box. The atmosphere was close, the two oil burners were radiating warmth, and the Christmas spirit tensed each one present.

Suddenly as "Mary" knelt before the infant, my son fell to the floor, his cane pole clattering on the varnished boards. The other two shepherds stepped suddenly away from him, probably sore afraid and embarrassed half to death.

The director hurried to him and lifted his sweaty head and said, "Where's his mother?" As soon as he fainted, I rose and immediately started toward him, but before I reached the platform two of the elders had him, one on each side, and lifted and walked him outdoors. I followed.

I wiped his clammy forehead with the head scarf. He said, "Whew! It got hot up there."

"Do you want to go home now?" I asked.

"Oh, no, let's go back in. I didn't get my treat yet."

Each year as I see children dressed in shepherd attire, I think of my shepherd who fell that December day at Bethlehem Church during the Christmas program. Bless his chubby little memory.

Several fragments of Christmas-church-related scenes spill over from University Church. The space of years and miles prevents clear focusing on the many Christmas programs at old U.C.C. But clear scenes from several remain.

For instance, it seems the front of the church represents an inn. A high school boy and girl are the innkeepers. She, too anxious to verbalize those memorized lines, said, "I wonder who's knocking at the door this time of night?"

He, trying to cue the off-stage knocker, and also attempting to present a sensible dialogue, put his hand to his ear and quickly responded, "I don't believe I hear any knocking—yet."

Needless to say, loud knocks sounded on the wall behind them and she repeated her lines as the audience smiled. The director sighed.

Then there was the time we crumpled brown paper sacks and scattered them over the platform. These were supposed to represent stones lying around the fields near Bethlehem.

A bashful girl, dressed in a long, white baptismal robe with attached tissue-paper wings, swooped on stage and accidentally kicked one of the stones out into the audience.

Before University Christian Church was remodeled, there was a small stage in the basement beside the baptistry. We rigged up a curtain from two bedspreads and gave a small Christmas presentation there. My youngest son, who was about six then, and another youngster were appointed to stand behind the curtains and draw them or open them as need be.

Prior to the program, these two young stagehands worked out fool-proof signals so that they drew or opened in smooth precision. But on that special night they had many coordination problems. Sometimes one half of the curtain would be open long after the other half had closed, and vice versa.

The two boys also presumably grew curious about the audience, as several times their heads appeared around the curtains for brief glances out. Imagine the ruffled composure of an angel saying importantly, "Fear not, for behold I bring you good tidings of great joy!" Then the smiles and the merriment as the two curtaidn pullers peeked around their posts.

Another time we thought an old chiming clock would add autheniticity to a farmhouse scene. Carrying the clock into the church disarranged its chiming accuracy, we found out too late to remedy.

15

The farm wife rocked and knitted and said, "My lands, here it is six o'clock. I must start supper." The clock registered six, to the plain view of all the audience, and it tightened up and began to chime—one time. That was fun.

The Christmas program at church is merely the culmination of weeks of preparation. Deciding what play to present, holding try-outs, choosing a cast, obtaining stage props, creating scenery, all the while keeping order and showing impartial interest in all concerned take numerous trips to the church. Usually work on the Christmas program starts immediately after Thanksgiving and only pure grit, prayer, and determination assure the goal—the program—of such frenzied activity.

The church bulletin carries the notice that the Christmas program will be held at a specific time, and miraculously all goes well on that appointed time. The hysterical laughing sprees, the late comers, the absentees, the prima donnas, the forgotten lines, all fade into a pleasant pattern.

The proud parents, grandparents, neighbors, and friends beam as brightly as Christmas lights twinkling in the sanctuary and each one is certain this is the best program ever presented. The small flubs and minute mistakes do not detract, but add human interest appeal.

I always like to think that the guest of honor at the Christmas program is the One whose birth is being commemorated. I like to imagine Jesus sitting there in a pew beside a beaming, loving parent, head bent a little sideways to hear the inarticulate toddlers, a smile on his lips and a fond twinkle in his observing eyes. I like to picture him laughing at the funny things and tears welling in his eyes when some poignant phrase touches a tender heart. I know he is experiencing the same emotions we feel.

He said, "Let the children come to me." He enjoyed their trusting presence, their frank and open looks, their guileless questions. I feel certain, then, that he comes to see the Christmas program.

I think He appreciates the hours of practice, the routine drill of memorization, the often outlandish costumes, as much as anyone. When I watch a young child deliver his "piece" in front of a group at church, I feel Christ's divine presence right there beside that child, blessing him, enjoying his company.

Jesus said, "Where two or three are gathered in my name, there am I in the midst of them." It reinforces my faith to believe, as I watch the Christmas program at church, that the loving Christ is right in the middle of the action, enjoying it as much as anyone.

Among my pieces of church-related Christmases are adult programs, too.

I see a cantata where we wore choir robes and carried lighted candles down the darkened aisle, then placed them in holders all along the front of the platform. Once I was chosen

to read passages between musical selections and had a problem knowing when to begin. The minister's wife played the organ for the program and I can see her gentle face in the candlelight yet, nodding for me to start reading. She played softly during the reading, a mere touch of melody, which haunts me after many years.

Many times refreshments were served after the Christmas program. The women went all out to create appropriate foods. We have made sandwiches cut like stars and trees, filled with green-tinted cream cheese. We have made cookies like candles and wreaths dotted with glittering candies. We have frosted cakes with green icing and studded red and green maraschino cherries about. We have added crushed peppermint candy to pale pink whipped cream and tinted coconut green and spelled out Merry Christmas to make the pieces of Christmas a visual treat.

When he lived physically on earth, he loved the fellowship of friends. He still does, and I know he's there if he have been fun things, special things, done with eager happiness to honor the anniversary of the birth of our Lord.

It is equally important that Jesus share the adult activities as well as the child-centered festivities. After all, church members are children of God, whatever their chronological age may be. I like to think of Jesus sampling a Christmasy-looking delicacy and making satisfied sounds of appreciation.

When he lived physically on earth, He he loved the fellowship of friends. He still does, and I know he's there if he received an invitation. Surely he was invited to the church's Christmas program, since he owns the church lock, stock, and barrel. He founded it, bought it back again, and, most important, loves it. It is natural for him to be there at the Christmas program as well as all other times.

I went to the car after some forgotten item one long-ago Christmas time. The parking lot was filled with snow-covered cars and the soft light shone through the big stained-glass windows of University Church. Snowflakes whirled past the glow and hit the red bricks of the building. I grabbed whatever I had gone to get and hurried back around the walk to the door.

Down the street, an automobile was stalled at the slick curb and suddenly sounded a snarl as vicious as an angered lion. After tire-spinning minutes it proceeded slowly down snowy Calvert Street, its twin taillights disappearing into the storm.

I shivered and entered the warm, friendly building where safety and sanity filled the blocky old church. Once upon a time Christians were tossed to the lions which snarled and devoured them. They had no appointed place to seek sanctuary. Perhaps the snarls and entanglements of modern day are warnings that lions still roam the land and Christians are in dire danger in the arena of living.

The Christmas programs at churches scattered throughout the world are seasonal touchstones to compare other segments of living. Personally, I think such programs are worth all the effort, time, and money involved. Little children are practicing more than lines in a sonnet when they deliver their Christmas "piece." They are practicing identity with self in the church and learning that Jesus wants them, needs them, and appreciates them.

They are making their own individual pieces of Christmas which they will take out, brush with memory's velvet touch, and relive and enjoy for many years far into the future.

> Churches are lit with luminous love
> And brightened with seasonal shine.
> Treats are far sweeter than ever before
> From church at Christmas time.

homes

Since this attempt to create an acrostic from the word "Christmas" is a gathering of my personal pieces of Christmas, the second letter stands for homes I've lived in.

The very first home I can remember at Christmas time was a small frame house. I lived there with my parents and toddler sister. The depression mercilessly squeezed the hope from Christmas and zero temperatures cut a deep chill over all.

I remember waking and feeling the cold and whimpering. My mother told me to get into bed with her. "Get in bed with us until Daddy gets the fire built, then you can get up and see what you got for Christmas."

I'd forgotten. This was Christmas!

I sprang from my bed, bare feet touching the icy floor and ran to our front room. There two kitchen chairs were set together in the middle of the room. On each was a pie pan filled with candies and in the center of each stood a little glazed-china doll. The dolls were about four inches long with movable arms and legs.

I stood on the cold linoleum and stared, shivering in my long nightgown so severely that my teeth clicked together. Then I grabbed a doll in each hand and ran to the bedroom to the warm, waiting snuggle in bed with my parents.

My little sister and I lay between our loving young parents, looking at the wonderful little dolls, moving their squeaking arms and wriggling deep in the depths of warm covers and love. I pressed my hard little doll under my cheek, then snuggled my head against my mother's cheek.

I was four and didn't know hard times existed. All I knew or needed was the loving presence of my family close about me. I was more content than a king.

That was my mother's last Christmas with us. Our home was divided the following March when Mother entered a sanitarium. We children were taken to our grandparents' home two hundred miles away to stay until she recovered. But she died the following May.

I am thankful I have that bright piece of Christmas to remember. It is one of the few memories I have of my loving mother and I cherish and thank her and thank God for her life.

My next home was the old house on the hill. Christmas, as well as all other days, was "slim pickin' " as my salty little grandfather said. One particular piece of Christmas memory of home glows with happiness yet. My father had written saying he would try his best to get home for Christmas. I remember listening to the train whistle as it came from the north, and hoping painfully that he would be on it.

The day before Christmas, my grandmother baked and cleaned and made preparation for the next day. My father surely would be here today, I thought. But the cold day crept on with slow, certain hours, the train whistles blew, but my beloved daddy did not come. I looked out the wavy windowpane toward town and watched darkness wrap everything from sight. I remember my reflection in the window and the image of my wizened grandparents, my sleepy little sister, and the tall lamp on the table. Emptiness made me feel physically ill. Despair shook my faith in my father and I felt hot bitter tears roll down my cheeks.

We went to bed early as usual and sleet hit the tin roof and sleep closed our eyes. I remember my grandmother saying, "Maybe your daddy will be here tomorrow."

When I awoke that Christmas morning I heard a strange, strong voice in the kitchen. I listened a minute, hardly daring to hope he was there.

I hurried to the kitchen and there sat my daddy. He opened his arms wide and I ran into the circle of them. He held me close and I was happy.

He brought gifts for all of us. There were identical little red brooms, two tiny flowered tea sets, two little dolls, and oranges, nuts, and candy in a red box.

I don't know how old I was that Christmas. Perhaps it was the first Christmas after my mother's death. That memory is a dear treasured piece of Christmas at home.

Christmases rolled on at the house on the hill and are blurred now and I am unable to fit the pieces together for each specific year.

There was the time we hung our long stockings on nails under the flue hole. I had told my sister I knew good and well that Grandma put things in them and planned to stay awake and see for sure. She agreed and we whispered and listened and grew sleepy.

Finally Grandma came with gentle feet to the chimney. I nudged my sister to come with me, but she was asleep. I stole from the bed, crept to the doorway, and saw my grandmother there in the firelight, her wrinkled face intent on her work. She filled the stockings from paper sacks of candy and oranges and nuts.

I stood watching, still in the doorway, and wished I was sleeping and had not seen. She turned when she finished and gasped at my presence. Trying to bluff through with humor, I said quickly, "What do you think you're doin', Mrs. Casey?"

"What do you think you're doin' out of bed at this hour?"

We both laughed quietly, she smacked my bottom in mock exasperation, and told me in a whisper to get back to bed.

My uncle and aunt and cousins brought gifts for Christmas to our old house on the hill. Aunt Elsie brought oilcloth for the table and it smelled new and felt slick to the touch. She once brought a dish filled with candy and told my grandmother that in the bottom of the dish were red and pink roses. I remember that I looked at her with doubt, but sure enough, when the candy was eaten, there were the promised roses, glowing in the dish.

My uncles made eggnog and drank it in the shanty near the coal mine because Grandma wouldn't allow liquor in the house on Christmas Day. She abhorred it at any time, but Christmas was a holy day, she said, and absolutely no liquor could be brought into her home.

We decorated the old house on the hill with popcorn and cranberry strings and looped paper. These were hung in the windows and draped over a little fire bush set in a cold room. We had no electricity, and Grandma was terrified of candles, so our dead little brown tree was thrust into a fruit jar and sat glumly, shedding dead particles for three or four days. It evoked the ire of Grandpa when he happened to stumble into it during the night and motivated Grandma to grumble at the dirt on the floor.

Christmas was indeed "slim pickin's" at my grandparents' home. Usually we had something extra for dinner, small gifts from exchanges at school and Sunday school, and occasionally, as the years passed, gifts from our father.

Christmas at home was special, however, because Grandma would get the old black Bible, settle down in the rocking chair beside the heating stove, adjust her glasses, and read from Luke the story of Christ's birth. Then she would explain it in her simple manner to our questioning minds.

These valuable pieces of Christmas at home made my childhood have meaning and purpose much more important than a great display of material wealth.

The first Christmas in my own home stands clear in my memory. I rearranged our sparse furnishings in the living room to make room for the tree at the window. We had a tall green tree and tree stand and white cotton bunting to spread around it. I placed new decorations of blue baubles and lights, and a star and glittering icicles shimmered evenly from each bough. Then I turned out all the lights except those on the tree and stood back and admired my first Christmas tree in my own home. How thankful I felt, how cherished my small home was!

Then I wondered how beautiful it must look to people going past and I quickly ran outside to see. I stood in the falling snow and gazed with wonder at the window which framed the Christmas tree.

My husband came home while I stood in the yard in the dark cold. His eyes must have widened when he turned in the driveway and the headlights swept over me.

"Why are you standing out here?" he asked.

"Looking at our tree," I said, shivering.

He put his arm around me and we stood for a minute together and looked at our first Christmas tree. Then we went inside and had supper and enjoyed the tree and our first Christmas together as a married couple in our own home.

God, bless all new homes, especially at Christmas time. Let the new bride and groom stand in admiration of the shining splendor of Christmas in their own home. Let the spirit of Christ be born anew and dwell in the new home. Let the sharing and the love go on all year as joyously as at Christmas time. Stand beside the new homes and embrace the homemakers and draw them closely together and draw them closely to you.

After children join the home, the pieces of Christmas grow chock full of beautiful patterns. There is no joy to equal the wondrous awe in the eyes of a child as he delights in each piece of Christmas. There is a reward when he plots to give Daddy a gift, when he hangs his stocking, when he sees the tree and when he opens his gifts. There is no plotting more deliciously pleasant than hiding presents and bringing them forth on Christmas Eve, quiet as fog, after the children are sleeping.

The myth of Santa was denied me as a child, as my grandmother felt Santa Claus and the reindeer had no place in the life of a Christian. She did not explain these feelings, she merely omitted such teaching.

I taught my children about Santa, probably as much for my own enjoyment as theirs. Personally, I feel that Christ shares the anticipation, the eager excitement, and the mystified magic of old Santa Claus. I do not think Santa should be taught to the exclusion of Christ's birth. I remember telling my first son

the story of the Baby Jesus and how the shepherds came and the angels sang and the wise men brought gifts to the Christ child.

He said, "And Santa Claus brought Baby Jesus a present." He was about three and I did not negate his idea.

Looking back now at the pieces of Christmas at home when my sons were babies, then little boys, then adolescents, then young men, I wonder where those Christmases were going that they raced so quickly past.

If I remember those noisy pieces of Christmas with a trace of maternal sadness because they are irrevocably gone, I cherish more dearly the pieces of Christmas at home I have now with little granddaughters. They restore the pieces as brightly as I wish.

The lights on the tree are dim compared with the light in their eyes. They look forward to coming to Grandma's on Christmas Eve and these pieces of time at home are most precious to me.

To mothers who rue and bemoan the absence of children, I'd like to say that, believe it or not, grandchildren are equally dear. Instead of the family growing smaller, it increases in size as the children grow up, leave the home, and establish homes of their own. There seems to me a special kind of Christmas sharing when daughters-in-law bring me a tin of homemade candy, or a special cake, or a mantle decoration, made with love exclusively for me. These are the necessary pieces of Christmas which enrich my segment of life, and I rejoice that my grown children are fast gathering pieces of Christmas in their own homes.

Christmas memories usually originate within the home. Certain unique customs are practiced through the years until those customs are taken for granted. At Christmas, I have always enjoyed a relaxed day. We do not have a big meal. We invite no guests and accept no invitations. Some Christmases have been spent napping, reading, eating when we chose to eat, and generally letting down on routine. We prepare ahead cake, pies, cookies, puddings, and usually a ham and potato salad, maybe cranberry salad and celery and cheese and a perking coffee pot. We eat as much or as little as often as we choose at our house. That is the way I like to enjoy my personal piece of Christmas at my home.

My home has Christmas decorations throughout, there are no shortages. For this I feel humble gratitude. Once in awhile I am tempted to leave the artificial tree in its box in the attic and go out in the country and hunt for a dried fire bush and drape it with popcorn and cranberry strings.

My family gives me beautifully wrapped gifts. We open them on Christmas Eve and I thank my sons and their wives and my two darling grandchildren and I love their choices. I appreciate every gift and thank them over and over and tell them they should have spent the money on themselves and not on me, and mean it sincerely.

I look at the finery and see many manifestations of love and goodwill toward me in my home. Yet I have never seen a small china doll about four inches tall; for some reason that would be a great package to open, or better yet, to find standing in a pie pan full of candy.

Some things remain amid a changing, rearranging, hurrying world. The biblical account of Christ's birth is still the beautiful and tender and lasting legacy that guarantees that the pieces of Christmas will remain forever and undeniably fit into a significant whole.

These words of Jesus' birth are Christmas. They hold together pieces of Christmas in the past and unite the pieces of Christmas now, all at home, because home is where there is love and caring. I read the account of Christ's birth and all my pieces of Christmas are sealed at home with a clear and protective and lasting patina.

> The home is such a busy place
> When Christmas time draws near.
> Home wraps a quilt of love about,
> And blots out every fear.

RETURNING

Why is the word "returning" included in my pieces of Christmas? What is returning? To whom are things returning? Where have they been? Why is there a return at Christmas time?

As the Christmas season approaches each year, the mail brings Christmas cards. These cards are from all over the country and from foreign lands. We get cards from people who have never been in our home, so it is not the person who is returning but the memory he has for us.

The practice of sending cards has become quite expensive and for some limited incomes even prohibitive. Yet, I cannot think of another piece of Christmas which brings more joy and

causes feelings of good will as effectively as receiving and sending cards.

I go to the mailbox in early December and thrill at the first Christmas card. I eagerly open it to see whose good wishes are returning to me another year. Some have included pieces of information bridging the space of one year and bringing me up to date on the happenings of someone who cared enough to remember me. Of course, the sender knew I cared enough to be glad to hear what had happened throughout the twelve months.

I tape the cards to the hall closet door and enjoy them again and again until New Year's. When the door becomes filled, I arrange them around the door frame into the living room and often across the bottom of the mirror. Then I appreciate and share my returning wishes with all who enter our home at Christmas time.

I find as much satisfaction from cards sent by nearby friends as I do from those which have come from far distances. It means that, although they may see me daily, they are sending a bit of thought my way—returning a portion of shared laughter, shared friendship. I joyfully accept it and cherish the thoughfulness and feel a close bond to the sender.

My Christmas card list has grown through the years. I am thankful for the friends I remember with greeting cards this year whom I did not know last year. I return a bit of the rapport we have known together and hope they will accept my card with the thought that I am returning a measure of me to them.

Although postage is expensive, addressing envelopes is time-consuming, and greeting cards which say just the right thing are often hard to find, the practice of receiving and sending Christmas cards is still an economical way to improve human relations and create attitudes of peace and goodwill toward those we love. I hope the practice does not perish, but will remain. The arrivals of Christmas cards are current pieces of Christmas returning to me to make my holiday whole.

Another thought about returning at Christmas time focuses on a local nursing home. The small group who live in the big rambling house on East Jackson Street was chosen by the Bible Club to be remembered on various holidays.

The teen-agers bought and wrapped small gifts and labeled each one with "m" for man, and "w" for woman. The home had seventeen patients last Christmas and each one had a gift.

We parked the cars at the service station on the corner and walked through the falling snowflakes to the home. We were gift-laden and had a good feeling because we were taking Christmas spirit to the old people.

The elderly ones received us with beaming smiles and expressions of happiness to see us again. They sat in arthritic positions and grasped the warm, young hands of the kids, tickled to death to share a piece of time with us.

The teen-agers were polite and showed friendly courtesy and the aged ones were happy that we had returned. We knew some of the regular ones and these spoke with fraternal intimacy. It seemed they wanted their fellow patients to know that we had been there before and had returned, and they looked forward to us returning again throughout the year.

We sang and served simple refreshments—remembering those with diabetic needs—and visited awhile. We left early because our old friends had early bedtimes. Clouded eyes watched with sparkling interest as the kids put on their coats and wished them a Merry Christmas.

I have always been amazed that the kids remembered and enjoyed these visits. Their eager voices prattled on and on about the patients. "Did you hear that old man sing?" "Man, what a voice!" "Did you see that little white-haired lady? The blind one? Did you see how she held on to her gift after I opened it for her?" "I thought I'd crack up when those two old men got into an argument over which carol we'd sing first."

I am most certain that returning to the home benefited the youngsters as much as or more than the old folks. The aged and infirm returned hospitality and cheerful appreciation to those of us who came calling on them. They gave a full return for each invested effort and made the kids look forward to returning. This piece of Christmas is bittersweet to me. The young and the old together, with me someplace in the middle. I would not choose to be a teen-ager again, nor do I choose to detour the required number of years to reach the favored status of old age. But the vivid contrast of these pieces of Christmas causes me to appreciate returning a measure of patience to the kids and to the old people. Both ends of the spectrum deserve it and need it and teach me something.

Each year at Christmas time when I unwrap the pieces of Christmas I have saved through the years, and hang them on the tree, I feel returning emotions. Some baubles evoke sadness, some love, some great, exuberant joy. The small blue ornaments have returned longer than all the others. These are the ones we bought for our very first Christmas. Several have been crushed, but five or six remain and return year after year. Although they were very inexpensive, they glow on the branches as importantly as those which bore a high price. These modest little baubles cause the feeling of new pride and adventure felt in our new home. They return year after year and reinforce the private privilege of having a home today.

All over the land are those whose plans include returning home for Christmas. Airline reservations are made. Letters and phone calls let someone at home and the someone away enjoy the anticipation of seeing that certain, special one returning for Christmas.

This past Christmas brought pieces of terrible weather. Winter decided to get rough and spew sleet from leaden skies and glaze the highways with treacherous ice. A neighbor couple drove fifty miles in the blizzard to the airport to meet a plane bringing their daughter home for the holidays. She came from across the country to spend Christmas at home.

The trip that ordinarily took an hour, took six. The anxieties felt on the late plane and the fears felt by those in the car, and later in the wait at the air terminal, were most unpleasant. But when the big plane landed and the worried faces relaxed, the fears were forgotten. The tedious trip home together was a shared adventure altogether worthwhile. When home came in view in the beams of the headlights in the dark, cold, swirling night, the whole dangerous piece of Christmas was suddenly safe and back to normal again.

There is something special about returning home at this special time of year. The weeks preceding and following Christmas might be much more favorable for travel. Yet, returning at the appointed time to share life with loved ones, is a dear piece of Christmas that is vital tradition, and that fits into the pattern in a meaningful way.

Other bright glimpses of pieces of Christmas glow on the scene and sparkle gray days. Santa Claus is an important celebrity returning to hold bashful children who sit lightly on his lap and lisp into his ear. The red mask may be sleazy, the white beard thin and straggly, but the joy in young hearts returns faith to the world of childhood.

Religious News Service

Ringing bells and clinking kettles return every Christmas and jangle the conscience of all who pass by. The coins collect and help the needy and bring returning awareness for those less fortunate. Deep gratitude returns for each blessing we have.

The rustling decorations of cities return year after year and swag over the street corners and blow in the snow. The time and money spent to put them up and take them down are seldom considered because the bright pieces of Christmas proclaim merry thoughts.

Christmas shopping returns in a frenzy of activity, the lists of necessities marked with thought and loving concern. Christmas parties and programs and gift swapping and caroling return and mark happy milestones as we remember the sweet pieces of Christmas of last year.

The mistletoe returns and dangles over the heads and invites shy lads to become suddenly bold. The yule log returns and blazes and crackles and casts rosy shadows and shoots sparks of gold. Bells return and reverberate gonging and pealing. People know the return of the good Christmas feeling.

Of course the most precious piece of Christmas returning is when we consider the first Christmas in old Bethlehem. As we return to the historical account in the Bible, we once again share the peace the shepherds knew, the joy the angels sang, the ponderous meditation the mother of Christ quietly and seriously felt. We return for a brief interval year by year to claim a measure of goodwill as a unique right and give a measure of peace toward our fellow planet travelers with hospitable hearts. hospitable hearts.

This is why "returning" is a needed piece of Christmas that the big, jumbled puzzle of life must have to be whole.

    Christmas Day, return in June,
    Don't wait till bleak December.
    Christmas Day, melt icy hearts
    Into warm and glowing embers.
    Christmas Day, if I should forget
    The tryst of your returning,
    A star will pierce the darkened world
    And set goodwill to burning.

Roger Lattner

innocents

Who are the innocents? Why are they included in my pieces of Christmas? It seems to me that Christmas is the personification of innocence because the innocent Christ child was born on the first Christmas Day.

The innocent ones are the children and the mentally deficient. The innocents are the helpless and defenseless who must be cared for by those who are no longer innocent.

Pieces of Christmas thoughts narrow in and finally focus on the blessed innocents whose guileless gaze brightens my life.

I can see a bright piece of Christmas when I remember my first son, eleven months old, reaching for the lights on the tree. I see his surprised expression when the green tree scratched his fat little hand. The wonder he showed, the light in his innocent, joy-filled eyes, made my pieces of Christmas sparkle with happiness.

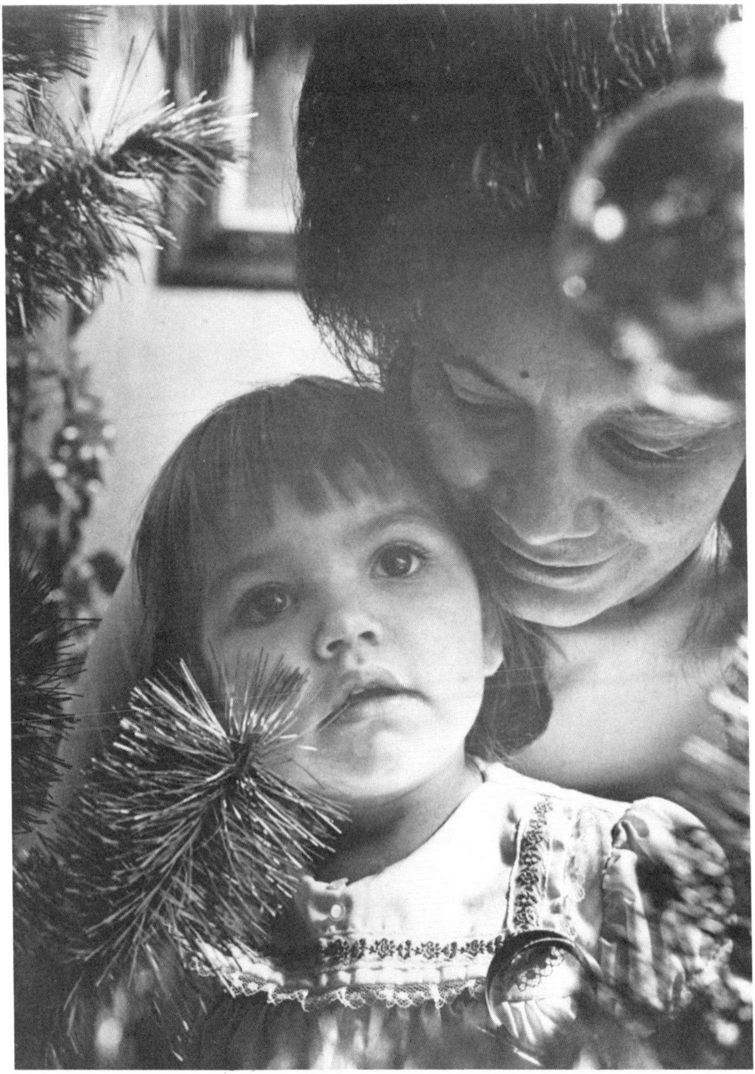

Religious News Service

Another related piece of Christmas fits into the niche of poignant memories. The time is a generation later and the innocent one is my granddaughter, first child of son number one. She was entirely too tiny, a wee little bit of a human, and about six weeks old. Thick black hair covered her round little head, and her doll-like hands reached into the warm air of the incubator. Tubes ran into her nostrils and were taped to various parts of her body to keep her alive.

Three perfect red roses adorned the shelf beside the incubator—a Christmas gift and symbol of love and unity as a family—parents with their first child.

We stood outside the glass and looked long at our little innocent one through the obstructions. Pain, concern, and acute compassion were in the eyes of my son. How different from my joyous piece of bright Christmas when I watched my first child toddle with curious health!

The artificial environment of the hospital, the small, warm incubator, the question "why?" is a sharp piece of Christmas that I'll never forget.

By the time her second Christmas rolled around, however, she, too, was a healthy, active toddler and the innocent gleam in her big, bright eyes made our happy hearts full. I thought backward one year and knew others were experiencing the same anguish we had known then.

I often wince because pieces of Christmas are often jagged and sudden sharp-cornered pieces pierce deeply into tender, love-saturated hearts.

Another precious piece of Christmas shows our second little granddaughter in a red and white stretchy sleeper outfit, not quite three weeks old. She came to Grandma's on Christmas Eve and gave and received gifts as importantly as anyone. We took pictures that evening as always before, and the one which I cherish shows my husband, holding this little sleeping child tenderly. His big arms hold the sleeping bundle of our innocent little one, cherished, protected, wanted, loved. A proud look of love shone bright on his face.

The babies are the innocents who teach us much in their trusting, dependent natures. If we who are older could rest as securely and completely in the arms of our heavenly Father as a young, innocent child rests in a loving father's arms, life would be simple. If we could cut through the complexities and rest on his promises without doubt and fear, we would know more freely his great love for mankind.

We must become as trusting little children before we can enter heaven. An innocent one three weeks old shows an example which we in all our wisdom should learn to emulate. Perhaps being a Christian entails a lot of unlearning and substituting trust for proof, faith for doubting, and a complete assurance for uneasy lives.

Our little sleeping granddaughter had nothing to fear in the arms of her loving grandfather. He held her carefully and would have died for her welfare, if need be.

That is what Christ did for us.

He shed his innocent blood in pain and disgrace and willingly died for our sins. We mark deep demerits when we refuse to admit and honor him into our lives.

The male babies who were slain by Herod's order are the acknowledged innocents. Imagine the pain these little ones felt to have their lives severed abruptly. Imagine their startled cries suddenly silenced into everlasting muteness. Imagine the grief-swollen hearts of the mothers. Pieces of Christmas hurt with their sharp, jagged edges. These little innocents suffered before the true Christmas picture could be exhibited to the world.

I like to imagine a large reserved space in heaven for these innocents. I like to picture Christ there with them, holding them, loving them, hearing and sharing their sweet laughter as pure as rain on a flower.

The holy innocents suffered greatly for the atrocious crimes of King Herod's anger and the innocent ones suffer yet. There are helpless infants who must suffer the needless abuse of adults, sometimes their own parents. This crime is equally infamous.

A book titled "Pieces of Christmas" suggests merriment and happy activities. Yet I must insert a piece of Christmas which necessarily hurts. If you who are reading this have a responsibility to a child, resolve this instant to accept your responsibility with the child's welfare first on the list of priorities.

Roger Lattner

Hold your little one tenderly. Don't jolt him. Don't drop him. Speak kindly to him, love him, adore him. He is just a tiny speck of humanity, but created by God. Cherish this little person and train him and care for him, not as a chore, but as a privilege. You are a huge giant to the little innocent one you hold in your arms. Have compassion on this child. He may be the one the world needs more than you would ever guess. You do not know what future you hold in your hands.

Treat your little innocent one with gentle attention and you will be rewarded each hour of the day. Do not be self-centered when it comes to considering your babies. Be kind to them, love them, touch their trusting forms gently.

A holiday has been set aside by some cultures to honor the martyred male children. It is called Holy Innocents Day or sometimes called Childermas Day. We cannot know with certainty how many children were murdered by Herod's angry, jealous command. The account is not given in the recorded word, yet we wince at the severity of such a cruel order.

Many little innocents are born with defective limbs and minds. Some lack the ability to survive. We wonder sometimes

Roger Lattner

what the purpose is of these aborted little people who presumably never had a chance. These are the innocents who will be blessed by the Father in heaven.

I cannot close my pieces of Christmas thinking of the innocents without one final thought. According to Matthew 18:5 "Whoever receives one such child in my name receives me." That is reward beyond measure and should be incentive enough to open all hearts to God's precious children.

Matthew 18:6 says: "But whoever causes one of these little ones who believe in me to sin, it would be better for him to have a great millstone fastened round his neck and to be drowned in the depth of the sea."

Acts of cruelty to innocent ones will not go unpunished forever. The child may overcome the fear and injustice and forget his persecutor, but the caring Father knows.

The innocent gaze of the Christ child, looking up from the nest of straw in a manger in busy old Bethlehem, pierced the awareness of God in the universe. Mary, young and untrained, loved this innocent baby. Her ponderous meditation about this innocent child causes us to identify with her awesome responsibility and to resolve to thank God for our little ones and care for them as if their lives depended on us, because they definitely do.

At Christmas time especially we think with love and benevolence toward the innocents. We cherish their lives and feel that Christmas is their special time. Pieces of Christmas are indeed sweet to the children, but their innocent lives deserve loving attention all the year through.

> Innocent baby hands reached into my heart
> And placed a gift of love there.
> God, please bless this innocent one,
> Is my heartfelt, continuous prayer.

Roger Lattner

songs

Pieces of Christmas would not be complete without the beautiful Christmas songs. Memories of Christmases past come hauntingly over the years on the gentle melodies of songs or carols.

Originally carols were danced. The carolers danced in a circle around a singer inside. Although carols were often sung and danced inside churches and cathedrals, they were not necessarily religious in content or in purpose.

Over the years, however, carols gradually centered around the life and birth of Christ and now we think of a carol as pertaining strictly to the Christmas season.

These songs of goodwill and cheerful, tender tunes float over December air as naturally as winter's snow. Christmas wouldn't be whole without the melodies of the carols, now sung to honor the nativity of Jesus, the Lord.

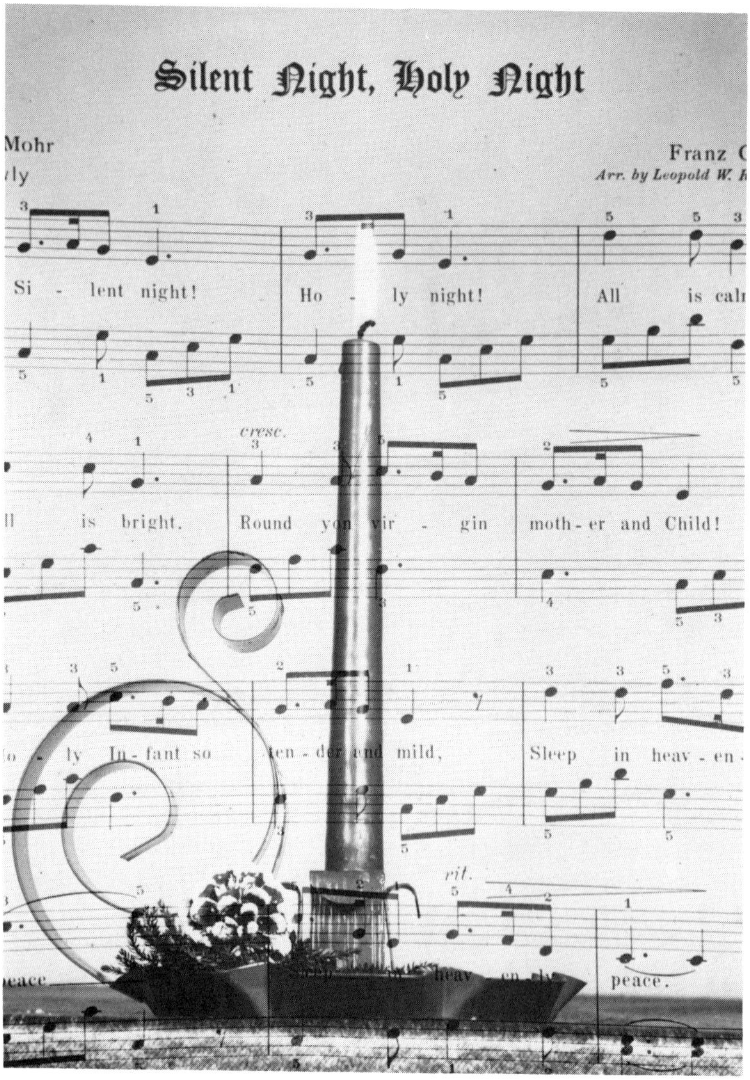
Silent Night, Holy Night
Mohr
Franz
Arr. by Leopold W.
Si - lent night! Ho - ly night! All is calm
is bright. Round yon vir - gin moth - er and Child!
ly In - fant so ten - der and mild, Sleep in heav - en
cresc.
rit.
peace.

My pieces of Christmas need the strains of "Silent Night" and "Away in a Manger" and "The First Noel" and many others to blend harmoniously through my Christmas memories. I love them all, but my favorite must be "Silent Night." This song was written by Joseph Mohr in 1818. He was twenty-six years old at the time and serving as an assistant minister in a small church in the village of Oberndorf, Austria.

The young minister wrote the words in a flash of pressurized necessity. It was the day before Christmas and Mohr had planned an appropriate program for the children at church. At this vital time, the organ suddenly broke down. Mohr, disappointed and probably somewhat disgusted, might have looked at the silent organ, perhaps hit it in desperation, as he dreaded the oncoming, embarrassing "stille nacht." He knew all were counting on him to make the event gala and happy and joyous.

Then, from inspiration born of necessity, he wrote the hauntingly beautiful words: "Silent Night, Holy Night, all is calm, all is bright."

He rushed his simple lyrics to the local schoolmaster, Franz Gruber, who composed the melody that very day. The music was set for two solos voices with guitar accompainment and was sung on that same Christmas Eve. In all likelihood Mohr and Gruber peered with apprehension at the singers and guitarist. They probably smiled in acute relief as they listened to the beautiful tune and meaningful words drift into the winter night and become a part of Christmas.

Well over a hundred years later, people still thrill at the quiet dignity of "Silent Night, Holy Night, Shepherds quake at the sight."

Children sing "Christ the Savior is born-n-n-n, Christ the Savior is born," and their skinny little necks strain and the cords in their throats quiver, and I listen to them and love them and hope fervently for their welfare. I cannot listen to children singing this song without feeling tears nearing and an ache in my heart. Although I have never voiced an appreciation to Joseph Mohr for writing about the birth of the Savior, I thank Him for the children who honor him and I also thank him for a young man and a silent church organ in a little church a long time ago in a faraway land.

The lovely little "Away in a Manger" is known by all and has an aura of mystery about it. The song first appeared in 1887 in James R. Murray's volume titled *Dainty Songs for Little Lads and Lassies.* It appeared under the heading "Luther's Cradle Hymn" and had been ascribed to Luther by most editors. Yet it was initialed by Murray. The odd thing is that neither lyrics nor melody bear the least resemblance to Luther's style; and that the little carol is practically unknown in Germany. In fact, it is known well only in the United States.

Richard S. Hill traced the origin of "Away in a Manger" and found the first appearance of the poem in a book called *A Little Children's Book* published in 1885 by the Evangelical Lutheran Church in North America. It was unsigned.

Even though it is not known who originally composed the beautiful song, everyone sings this soothing lullaby and is hushed by the words, "The little Lord Jesus, asleep in the hay."

The list of songs which are sung at the Christmas season is very long. The pieces of tune, fragments of melody, and bars of music fit into a pattern, much needed to complete the finished picture made from assorted pieces of Christmas.

"Jingle Bells" is associated with Christmas, but in reality has no specific reference to Christmas. John Pierpont wrote the words and the music and children love to sing the lusty tune. "Jingle Bells" has become a rollicking part of our Christmas carols.

"Joy to the World" also lacks a definite reference to Christmas, but is primarily sung at the Christmas season. The words to this song based on Psalm 98 were written by Isaac Watts. The melody, reminiscent of the 18th-century fugue, is credited to Handel. However, the true authorship of this hymn, too, is questionable. The hymn first appeared in an English hymnal in 1719.

Another well-known and often-sung carol with an ambiguous origin is "Oh, Come all Ye Faithful" or "Adeste Fidelis." It is acknowledged to be the work of John Francis Wade, who worked as a copyist in France. Even though manuscripts were intialed by him, the words could have sprung from the inspiration of an anonymous Frenchman. Others say the composer was probably an Englishman, John Reading. Although there is doubt concerning the author and the composer, all will agree that the song is definitely joyful and triumphant to every faithful person who sings or listens to Christmas songs. Here it is that we are instructed to "Come ye, O come ye to Bethlehem." In reality our thoughts return to the little city of David where the Christ infant entered into the hearts of mankind.

"O Little Town of Bethlehem" introduces that beautiful little hymn written by Phillips Brooks, a highly respected bishop of Massachusetts. When he was thirty, he visited the Holy Land and rode horseback from Jerusalem to Bethlehem shortly before Christmas. This event is said to have inspired the verses written over one hundred years ago.

The church organist, Lewis H. Redner, composed the setting for the words and the song made its debut at Christmas services in Holy Trinity Church in Philadelphia where Brooks was rector.

Thoughts of beauty, comfort, solace sometimes spring from hurting hearts. Henry Wadsworth Longfellow heard bells on a Christmas Day and from a grief-stricken heart wrote the poem, "I Heard the Bells on Christmas Day." He never intended it to be sung and it is evident his thoughts were far from singing. His son, a lieutenant in the Army of the Potomac, had recently received a serious injury. The grieving, worried father father poured out his ultimate despair with these poignant words in the third stanza:

> And in despair I bowed my head;
> "There is no peace on earth," I said,
> "For hate is strong and mocks the song
> of Peace on earth, good will to men."

The melody, originally known as ILLSLEY was one hundred and fifty years old when Longfellow wrote the poem. It is not known who first used the melody with these lyrics.

The song is a ready reminder that the sounds of Christmas Day, though traditionally joyous, often peal on hollow sadness. Yet it is the familiar sounds and familiar carols which give a sense of order, peace, and continuity to a rampant world. Beautiful melodies unobtrusively help to repair the broken pieces of Christmas.

The most popular Christmas solo ever written was denounced by the French because of "its lack of musical taste and total absence of the spirit of religion." This song is "O Holy Night." As we hear the inspiring and reverent words translated by John S. Dwight over one hundred years ago, we wonder at the severity which could criticize such adoration. We sing the words and are thankful that the holy night brought the Holy Child and also that the song rose high above the false stigma about it.

Matthew and Luke record the events on the night of Christ's birth, and to these records many Christmas songs allude. Angels, stars, voices from high places find the way inside sacred songs. The second chapter of Luke inspired "It Came Upon a Midnight Clear." An American author, Edmund H. Sears, a graduate of Harvard Divinity School, wrote the words and Richard S. Willis, from Yale, composed the melody. It was published in 1850 and it is doubtful that these men ever met. The "glorious song of old" unfolded peacefully and continues to bring "peace on earth, good will to men" each Christmas time.

"Angels We Have Heard on High" to the tune GLORIA has a legend that says a second-century Pope, Telephorus, ordered the song sung at midnight mass each Christmas Eve. Some doubt the logic of the saying because according to style the song did not appear before the eighteenth century. The chorus lends itself well to beautiful and easy harmony. The verses have always sounded quaintly Oriental to my untrained musical ear, but it is thought the song came from France.

Another pastoral scene is word sketched in the song "While Shepherds Watched their Flocks by Night," written by poet laureate Nahum Tate. The melody is adopted from Handel's opera *Siroe*. This song was the only Christmas hymn officially sanctioned by the Church of England for use in divine worship services.

Another Bible-related song is "Hark, the Herald Angels Sing" written by Charles Wesley with Mendelssohn as the composer. He thought "the music would never do for sacred words." Both author and composer had died long before the lyrics and the melody were joined. It seems a little ironic that we can enjoy this song while the creators never had the opportunity to know the satisfaction it gives to singers and to listeners.

The numbers of Christmas songs are legion. In addition to those synonymous with the church and honoring Christ's birth, are numerous ditties about Santa and snowmen and reindeer on the roof, and little Nell's stocking. This essay on Christmas songs has necessarily been limited with the primary emphasis on reverent songs. All serve a purpose, but it is ob-

Unicef

vious that the songs of adoration have never grown old, as the custom often is for the more secular songs. For example, Nahum Tate, the Englishman who wrote "While Shepherds Watched Their Flocks" lived from 1652 until 1715. His words are repeated year after year over the centuries and have no conceivable end. Many popular, secular songs are heard for a few years and die from lack of attention.

"We Three Kings of Orient Are" sounds medieval, but was written by John Henry Hopkins, Jr., who died in 1891, comparatively recently. Hopkins, a brilliant young man, was the son of a Vermont Bishop, and designed stained-glass windows in his spare time. Perhaps the symmetry of delicate-hued panes inspired Gaspar, Melchoir, and Balthasar. Whatever the spark of inspiration, these three kings have prophetically "come from afar."

"What Child Is This?" comes from England. Its tune, GREENSLEEVES, dates from the seventeenth century. The words now sung to answer the ancient question, "This, this is Christ the King, the Babe, the Son of Mary" were written about 1865 during Queen Victoria's reign.

A Negro spiritual sung at Christmas commands "Go Tell It on the Mountain . . . That Jesus Christ Is Born!" This is a Christmas song in every sense of the word and is sung by all Christian peoples today.

As we listen to Christmas songs, whether at church, or grouped around a piano at home, we know without a doubt that Christmas has come again. Often the frenzied mood of the season saps the strength. Shopping, baking, wrapping,

Roger Lattner

planning are enjoyable tasks, to be sure, but do tire the strongest at times. The soothing sounds of Christmas songs refresh and renew as the ancient words and dignified melodies permeate our lives.

My pieces of Christmas memories compel me to give "songs" an important, special priority. In my mind's eye I see my Sunday school class of teen-agers when we went through the snowy roads about six miles east of town and sang carols to a dear friend unable to attend church for some time. We had planned to stand on her porch and sing, but she insisted that we come inside. She gripped our cold hands and gave us steaming cocoa and freshly baked cookies. Tears came to her eyes as she thanked us for coming.

The kids are adults now and are scattered far and wide. But each year the same words, same tunes, same sentimental feelings come rushing through the winter cold and serve the unique purpose of warming hearts admirably again and again.

There are other classes of teen-agers, there are other adult shut-ins, and we sing the old songs in different blends year by passing year. We always leave with, "We wish you a merry Christmas! We wish you a merry Christmas! We wish you a merry Christmas, and a Happy New Year!"

> Silent air, dark, clear,
> Sparkling stars, heaven-near,
> Sudden voices blending dear
> In the bittersweet songs of Christmas.
>
> Angels bend to better hear
> As untrained voices know no fear
> Because we sing these songs each year,
> The sweet-sad songs of Christmas.

traditions

As the winter season approaches, various activities take an imperative place in our society. Most of us never stop to consider why we put up a tree, why we hang mistletoe, and stockings, or why we call a huge log for the fireplace the "Yule log" only at Christmas time.

Many know the answers, but I have long assumed that most of these Christmas traditions mysteriously sprang into existence somewhere back in time for the express purpose of giving joy to the children. After doing just a little research, I now know more about the "why" factor and can more fully appreciate their joyous purposes.

Probably the most widespread tradition is that of decorating a tree. If we look at this activity in a purely practical aspect, we must admit that cutting a small tree is a waste of natural resources. When we consider that evergreens are cut by the thousands to be looked at for a few days and then discarded,

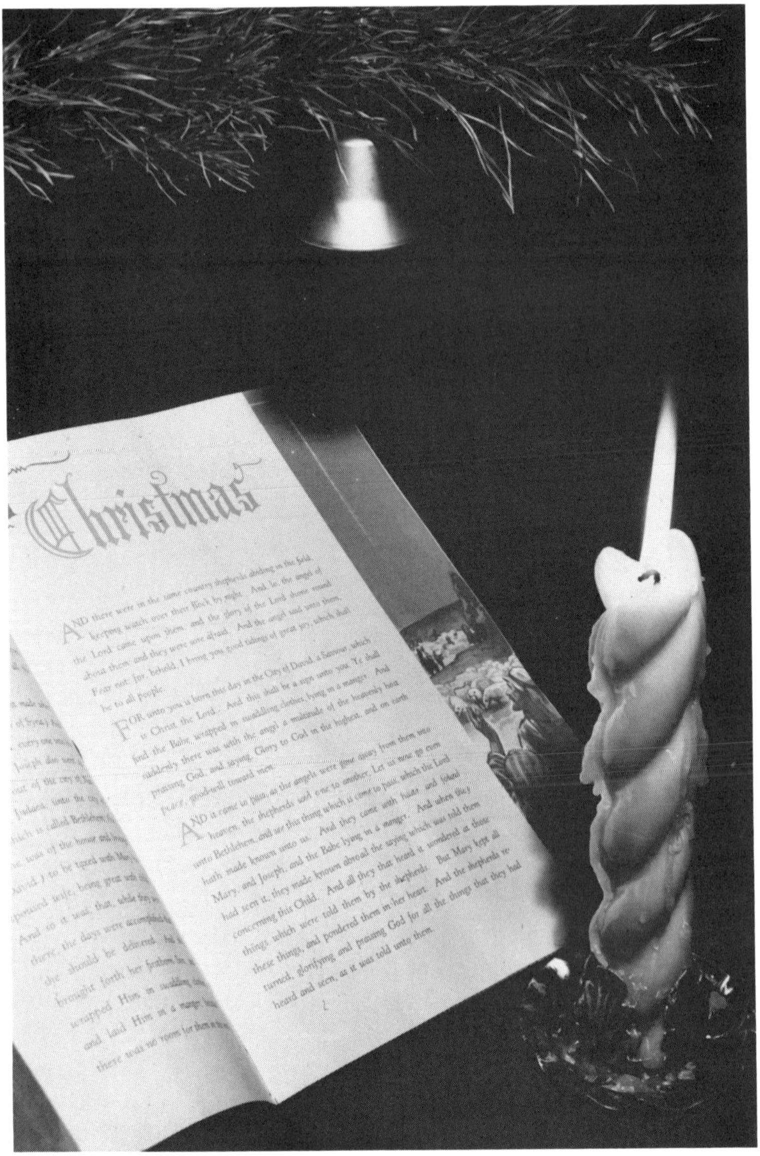
Christmas

the waste seems inexcusable. When we think about disposing of these dried, tag-end-icicled trees, we add another uncomplimentary activity by either burning it, or paying someone to haul it away. Then we must consider that it often takes valuable space in our homes and sheds needles on the carpet, which in turn clog the sweeper.

Added to the negative view of the Christmas tree is the danger factor. Costly fires break out due to faulty and/or overloaded circuits and the dried tree is ready tinder for the slightest spark.

Yet, in spite of all the logical reasons why we should omit the bother of the tree each Christmas time, we will continue to select one, pay a huge price for it, transport its unwieldy shape home, decorate it, and most important, enjoy it. My individual pieces of Christmas demand a tree to illumine the living room for a few days and illumine our lives for another holiday season.

Christmas is the celebration of the birth of Christ, as any child knows. Why then, do we put a tree in the house, of all places? Surely that action has no relevancy to the birth of the Christ child.

Admittedly the use of the Christmas tree originated as a pagan practice. Long, long ago, shrouded in the mists of ambiguous time, people worshiped trees. They adorned them with various baubles. The Maypole rites are related to the idea of tree worship.

European legends tell of the trees bursting into bloom with fully ripened fruit on Christmas Eve. Perhaps this is why we today decorate our trees with bright, fantastic "fruits" of every hue.

A Christ-related legend tells that Joseph of Arimathea stuck his staff into the ground and it grew and blossomed into a beautiful living tree. This legend originated in England and who is to say whether or not Joseph came to medieval England and actually imbedded a sprout into the earth, perhaps as a marker, and it grew and sprouted leaves, and later bloomed and bore fruit. Although the idea is farfetched, it is possible.

The bleakness of ancient European winters was relieved by potting small trees during the summer season, carrying them inside before frost, and caring tenderly for them. The branches often grew and ran along the ceiling. Along about Christmas time, these trees would burst into forced bloom and thus became known as Christmas trees.

For those who lacked easy access to living trees, and perhaps lacked green thumbs as well, artificial decorations

Suzanne Pickens

served as satisfactory substitutes. Year by year the desire to brighten the home at Christmas grew, until it seemed the natural thing to do.

The idea of a Christmas tree as we know it, originated in Germany and is comparatively new. It has been told that Martin Luther looked up into the starshine of heaven, and grateful for the gift of God's Son, went inside and decorated a tree with shimmering candles to simulate the star-studded sky dome.

Luther, the pillar of the Reformation, showed more romantic adoration than did his follower, Calvin, who objected to the secular Christmas tree.

The Christmas tree custom grew slowly in many lands, but surely, until by the middle of the nineteenth century, its presence was taken for granted. Paris initiated the Christmas tree in 1840. Queen Victoria ordered one set in Windsor Castle in 1841, and from then on the Christmas tree was guaranteed a respected place in England.

Gradually the once wholly secular practice was introduced into the churches and now softly glowing evergreen trees are a welcome part of the religious services in many churches. The constant color which never changes seems a fitting memorial to the birth of the One who is the same yesterday, today, and always.

The home without a Christmas tree seems sad. The glowing tree provides a valuable piece for the Christmas picture to portray the joys of the season. Many homeowners decorate shrubbery outside. Twinkling limbs etched against dark winter skies now glitter all across the land. Cities swag evergreen boughs at corners and lamp-posts and place lights within the greenery. The Christmas tree is the expected sight at all places at the holiday season and we gladly endure the inconveniences because we feel they are altogether worthwhile.

Another traditional practice is the hanging of the greens. This is akin to decorating a tree. The symbolic green of life suggests the One whose life is never ending.

The holly and ivy, now considered traditional Christmas garlands, were used in wintertime religious festivities by medieval Druids. A rural English superstition held that if the holly brought into the house at Christmas time was rough and rugged, the husband would be the master. If the holly leaves were smooth, the wife would be the dominant partner.

The Welch carol, "Deck the Halls with Boughs of Holly," might have arisen from this tale of ancient folklore. We can imagine the jolly laughter as young couples looked at the holly leaves to see which one would rule the house another year.

Holly is said to be the hiding place of small, friendly fairies, who love the holly so much that they remain hidden in the leaves even after it is cut and brought inside. These beings blessed the homes where holly was hung and prevented evil spirits from entering. Sometimes a sprig would be tacked over the barn door to ensure goodwill to the animals. Legends of folklore tell that the farm animals knelt on Christmas Eve when holly adorned the barn door.

Mistletoe is hung in doorways and invites a kiss for those who happen to walk under it. This popular tradition sprang from a solemn pagan practice which originated in England. The parasitical mistletoe, guidhel, or all-heal, as it was known, was a symbol for love and peace. At certain times of the year, a solemn procession went into the woods and found the mistletoe growing on the largest oak tree. The arch druid climbed the tree and cut the mistletoe free. It fell into a large, taut cloth held by a group of young women. Sacrificial services followed, then the mistletoe branches were cut into small segments and given to each one present as a token of goodwill. These were placed in doorways and in addition to advising all visitors that the host was a peaceful man, they were thought to have special, magic, curative powers.

Sometimes warring soldiers came upon a bough of mistletoe in the woods and at the sight of it, immediately declared a truce. The plant became synonymous with peace and goodwill. Often these characteristics were manifested with an embrace or a kiss to declare to the visitor that he was a welcome guest.

Evidently the plant has no actual relevancy to the birth of Christ. Yet it seems that those who love the Lord can always draw analogies representing some Christian aspect.

The mistletoe has no roots in the earth, but draws its sustenance from the life of another plant. The roots delve into the slow-yielding cells of the host tree and slowly but surely kill it. We might compare the love of Christ permeating every area of life, until we die to self and give ourselves completely to the One who loves the most.

Another old tradition popular with young people aware of the opposite sex, is that of peeling apples. Young ladies peeled a large, shiny red apple carefully, leaving the long strip of peeling in one piece. Then they tossed this over their shoulders and looked to see whose initial the peeling formed. Perhaps this is why red apples are often called Christmas apples.

Burning the Yule log is another traditional practice. This ancient pagan custom also sprang from England and as Christianity spread, the church allowed this activity to continue as a Christmas custom. Originally the huge log was burned as a dedication to the light of the world—the sun. In Christian thoughts, the dedication is to the Light of the World—the Son.

As the carefully chosen, ritualistic log burned, vows of friendship were renewed, quarrels forgiven, and optimistic dreams shared by those reflected in the light of the Yule log as they basked in its warmth.

Christmas needs every available piece of appropriate custom to ensure the Light of the World, Jesus, to live and to warm the cold and often hostile hearts of mankind.

Bells ring out on Christmas Day and peal their echoes across the land. The tradition of bells at Christmas is taken from antiquity and is linked with pagan and Christian practices.

Christmas was a well-established holiday before the ancient bells were heard inside the church. Now bells are expected in all Christendom. Bells were thought of so highly they were hoisted to the highest possible place and given the privileged position. Many churches grace the countryside, their steeples pointing toward heaven with a bell, safe in its special niche, ready to ring out the tidings.

Bells were once the media whereby all who heard were informed. The glad, clamorous sound brought merriment and laughter, the slow tolling sounds brought sadness.

My own personal pieces of Christmas include the sound of the church bells as I walked with my grandmother and sister toward the church one Christmas Eve. We heard the bells every Sunday morning, their pealing inviting and warning that time was slipping by! But this was night and not even Sunday and the bells were a special novelty. We walked single file down our hill path, starting for the Christmas service. The moonlight whitened the gleaming landscape in a type of dream world and the gonging bells seemed to come from some heavenly source. We walked the three miles, through the village, and stamped the snow from our feet on the steps before the church right under the bells.

    Santa Claus is a tradition brought from Holland. There he was known as St. Nicholas, a good bishop, and rode a white horse. The children set their wooden shoes outside the door, filled with hay for the horse, and in return St. Nicholas left gifts in the shoes.

Once, it has been told, St. Nicholas dropped a purse down the chimney of a certain good peasant. A stocking hanging at the fireplace, caught the purse. Thus the tradition of hanging a stocking at the fireplace on Christmas Eve came about. Probably this legend had a kernel of truth, as do most legends, as many people in early times before the days of central heating hung various items of apparel by the fire to be able to dress more comfortably the next morning. Today it is fun for the children to hang their stockings and wait eagerly to see what surprises Santa will bring.

Every land has its native Christmas traditions. These are varied and strange to all except those who know them. Many, many plants, flowers, and trees carry intricate, mysterious legends pertaining to Christmas folklore. Many traditional Christmas foods and beverages have interesting stories connected with Christmas. An interesting book could be written on any facet alone as the information is profuse.

Christmas has been celebrated at different times and supposedly no one knows the exact date of the Christ child's birth. Too much is not known about the nativity, but enough is known to celebrate it with merry hearts and joyous optimism.

In our country, Christmas is the number one holy day. Even the Jewish people respectfully honor those who honor the day. Yet as late as 1659 the General Court in Massachusetts fined anyone found observing Christmas in a festive way five shillings.

The Christmas present was not always so. Christmas was slow to become recognized in many places, but children needed Christmas to teach them the spirit of giving, loving, and looking forward to a cherished dream. Grownups need to become as little children in these respects. We need the old traditional practices because they link us to the past and tie us to childhood and prepare a basis for future generations.

> Ring the bells, trim the tree,
> Light the fire, and sing a carol.
> Traditions bring Christmas back to me
> And also to others across the sea
> Uniting the world in joyous apparel.

MORNING

Pieces of Christmas must include the culminating, completing factor—morning. Christmas morning is the time long-hoped-for and looked-forward-to in impatient anticipation. Morning is the beginning, looking ahead to a new and happy day.

Christmas morning is magic in every sense of the word. That first Christmas morning the magic was manifested in the form of the Christ child, the holy Infant, Jesus, wrapped and swaddled in soft cloth and adoring love. Mary knew the sense of wonder as she cared for her baby timidly and gently under difficult, makeshift conditions.

There is much we cannot know with certainty about Christ's young mother, Mary. Her age has been presumed variously, possibly the midteens is usually accepted. Whatever her exact age, we can only bow in humble, appreciative adoration to this young woman who fulfilled God's purpose in her youth.

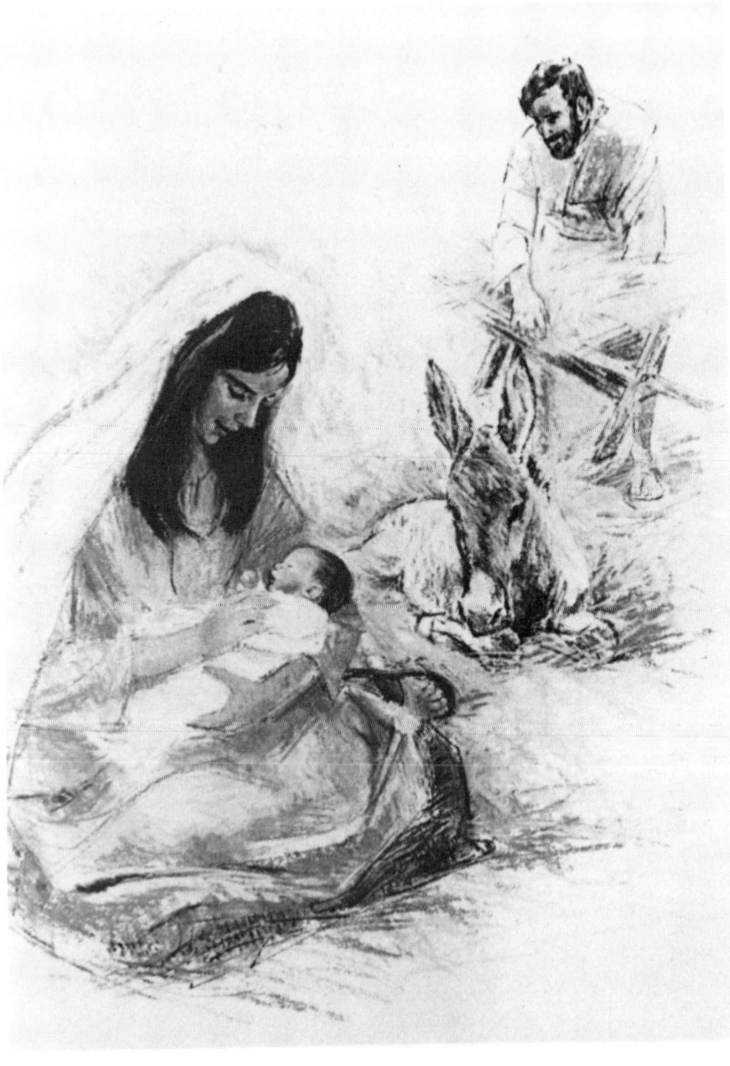

Religious News Service

Because she was young and without experience, many have inferred that she was an unthinking person. This cannot be true. The exact opposite has more evidence. If a young woman, soon to be delivered, felt compelled to accompany her husband on an important journey, much more prudent planning would be needed than if she expected to "take it easy" at home. I wonder who, besides young, thoughtful Mary, provided the swaddling clothes which she wrapped about her baby. Obviously she did.

Let us imagine Mary, heavy with child, preparing the necessary items to include on their trip to Bethlehem. I can picture her, busy and sure, as she wondered what she should take along. Perhaps she thought she and Joseph would be back home before the baby arrived, but just in case, she made provision to care for her child and herself.

Young as she was she bravely completed the prophecy spoken centuries before. In the morning at Bethlehem, she held the reason that Christmas exists.

That morning, special and majestic to a few, was commonplace to many. That morning heralded a new day which promised continual mornings. That morning, with soft air and new light, came after a night of anxiety, rejection, pain, and bedazzled heavenly chaos. That first Christmas morning brought calm and wonder and peace and rest to the young mother as she lay still with her child.

Christmas morning today marks the end of thoughtful, careful planning. Preparations have been made long before the anticipated, long-awaited morning. Christmas morning is often filled with chaotic haste and bedazzled excitement, nearly as loud in child-filled homes as the songs of the angels. But the early morning hours quiet down to the calm and happy, most beautiful time of the whole year, Christmas morning. This is the way it is for some, yet there are many who think the day is commonplace and ordinary.

As I think of a panorama of Christmas mornings, I see my sons lying on the floor around the tree, playing with toys that Santa brought. I see crumpled paper and meandering ribbons, I see myself smoothing the papers and winding the ribbons and putting a bit of order into our home. I see boxes of candy and well-filled stockings and plenty of food, prepared ahead for Christmas morning. I see new sleds and warm wraps and soft-footed pajamas and warm, clean, comfortable surroundings. For these gifts, I humbly and most gratefully thank the beneficent God.

Christmas morning brings a new light, a new awareness that my traditional, stereotyped Christmas morning is not shared by countless multitudes. As I enjoy the peace of Christmas morning, I feel a tinge of sadness that there are children whose feet are cold, whose eyes are searching in vain, and whose stomachs are bloated from lack of nourishing food.

These facts are what make my own personal pieces of Christmas sharp, jagged, and heart-piercing. If the magic of Christmas morning could ensure each child a gift of happiness, then all the pieces of Christmas would fit comfortably into a whole and lovely pattern.

What can we do? How can we help? Where do we start? These questions are without total answers. Giving Christmas happiness is the sole objective of many agencies. Countless individuals spend much time, thought, and money to ensure that neglected little ones are not forgotten. This is a commendable work, though far from complete, as we consider the masses of needy children.

If each of us started with one, just one, to bestow the gift of a joyous Christmas morning, our own joy would be much deeper. Sometimes we develop the mistaken idea that since we can't afford much, we need not bother with anything. We have the idea that it takes a lot of money to make even one child's Christmas morning a happy time.

I know from past experience this is not true. I remember a Christmas morning when my gift was a twenty-five-cent book. It was wrapped in green tissue paper and tied with a red ribbon and had my name on the tag. I still can remember the thrill of unwinding the wrapping and gazing in wonder at the pages of a book that was given to me by a teacher. That book was a Shirley Temple book and I was transported to a world I never knew existed as I looked with rapt attention at the beautiful pictures. That gift gave me great satisfaction and made my Christmas morning a very happy time.

It does not take much to make a child happy. A coloring book and a box of crayons, a set of water colors and some sheets of white paper, paper dolls and a small pair of scissors, a jar of paste and some construction paper as well as a book with the name of the child written in it will work wonders. This is what makes Christmas morning such a special piece of life. We get to open or unwrap something that is ours and ours alone—something that was bought, wrapped, and given specifically to us because someone cared enough to give us a gift.

Religious News Service

It seems that is what Christmas morning is all about—wrapping up a piece of concern for someone else and giving it in a spirit of love and goodwill. It seems the first Christmas morning was a synthesis of all the Christmas mornings to follow—Mary tenderly wrapping God's gift of concern and giving that gift, a part of himself, in a spirit of love and goodwill to all mankind. Even though that most priceless Gift was presented to all the world, it represents a thoughtful, personal, specific tribute to each one individually.

Morning of Christmas Day represents the climax of hopes, dreams, and plans. This is the revelation of a year-long plot which unfolds systematically over the preceding months. Christmas morning develops an appreciation of setting, character, tone, and purpose. Christmas morning is a discovery after hours, days, and weeks of suspense. Most of all,

Christmas morning is a love story filled with pieces of Christmas exquisitely and painfully sprinkled deep in my heart.
>
> Christmas morning, here at last
> With gifts of love, new gleaming.
> Christmas morning, so soon past,
> And kept safe for future dreaming.

angels

We can't think Christmas very long without thinking of angels. According to the Christmas story a host of angels, sang hallelujahs over the fields near Bethlehem the night that Christ was born. Angels, therefore were the first to introduce the Christmas message.

When I decided on an acrostic format made from the word "Christmas," I didn't hesitate an instant to choose "angels" for the "A." When I began to evaluate what I knew about angels, however, I discovered I knew very little.

All Bible-reading peoples are familiar with angels. An angel appeared to Mary to announce that she had been chosen by God to bear his Son. An angel came to Joseph and eased his troubled mind about the innocent Mary's virtue. An angel warned Joseph and Mary to flee into the safety of Egypt and advised them when the danger had past. Angels ministered to Jesus after his trying, tiring forty-day period in the wilderness.

Roger Lattner

We read that angels rolled the stone from Christ's tomb and acted as courteous agents to the women who came calling sorrowfully. Other than these well-known incidents, there are other biblical references to angels. Angels appeared many times in Old Testament writings. Angels are mentioned in Acts, Hebrews, 2 Thessalonians, and Revelation. They are not strictly limited directly to Christ, as we usually think.

Angels are mentioned so often and so specifically that we cannot shrug off the word as a typical, current figure of speech. What, or who, then, actually are angels? Where do they exist? What is their purpose? How do they appear? Why are angels needed?

The Bible and a Bible Commentary and an encyclopedia give some answers, yet I am amazed that so little information is readily available for the general reader. I found that a science called "angelology" exists, and I humbly apologize for my lack of research which should have been a prerequisite before attempting to write about angels. Yet angels definitely have a plan and a place even for those of us who know little about them. Angels fill one piece of Christmas importantly.

The word "angel" from the Greek and from the Hebrew means simply "a messenger." Other terms for God's messengers are "sons of God," and "sons of the mighty," "watchers," "mighty ones," and "holy ones." The expressions "host of heaven" and "host of the Lord" suggest an enormous number of angels. Two are named specifically in the Bible: Gabriel and Michael. Michael is called the archangel. We find angels exists from Satan as well as from God. Since the word means "messenger," it is logical to assume that both good and positive or bad and negative forces must send messengers to spread their doctrine to uninformed ones.

Angels are supernatural personalities of the invisible world. Many churches acknowledge the presence of angels openly; other churches profess a belief in angels, but ignore a direct or specific explanation. Some church groups feel that angels appeared and counseled somewhere back in ancient Bible times, but are obsolete nowadays.

Many of the ideas about angels have come from art and literature, especially Milton. These descriptions are subjective with their creators. Although the Bible does not teach that angels have wings, this idea is generally pictured when an angel's appearance is invoked.

Abraham of old entertained angels and never dreamed they were sent from God until after they had gone. We now entertain angels and think they are treasured friends, which in truth they are. Jacob wrestled with an angel in a terrible conflict. Perhaps we should look respectfully at those who wage battles with us. Perhaps they have been sent from God.

It seems to me that those who love God and tune in on his frequency have a divine mission while on this space ship, Earth. I think destiny decrees that certain people will meet, and though the meeting may be brief, a divine mission is accomplished.

Who are my angels, the messengers sent from God to me? Sometimes near Christmas, I hear their glad tidings of great joy over the radio. Their voices are heard in exquisite harmony as we drive down today's highway. The high clear tones tell me there is "Peace on earth, goodwill to men." Angel voices hum from spinning disks as I listen to Christmas recordings. I hear the high, thin sound of "The Little Drummer Boy" and realize that a message from God commands me to give a gift to the Lord I adore. I learn from this song that he wants my native abilities, no matter how insignificant they appear to me. Angel voices harmonize with the words of "White Christmas" and God's message is clear that I should appreciate my home, my children, and the special intimacy of many shared Christmases.

Perhaps those who sing Christmas songs do not realize their angelic mission. Yet if we who hear receive a good message from the singing, we might accurately call the bearers Angels, messengers of God.

The biblical angels appeared at various times other than Christmas, and indeed appeared before the event existed. Current angels also make visitations throughout the year.

Those who do rescue work not only perform appointed duties, but miraculously swoop in and evacuate those in danger. A pilot, hearing a distress call far over the ocean, turned the big plane, kept in communication with the ailing plane, and found it. It seems a miracle that from the hidden expanse of darkness, two planes could meet, connect, and one receive needed fuel from the other, high over the cold ocean.

The two pilots never met, never knew each other, but one came from invisible places and ministered to one in need and such is the purpose of scriptural angels.

As the space crews returned to earth, perhaps they thought of the rescue ship and hovering helicopter as carrying a host of ministering angels, ready to snatch them back to earth's safety.

As firemen appear amid leaping flames, their presence is viewed entirely angelic by those trapped and helpless. A tanned and able lifeguard who saves a drowning person is also functioning as an angel, a messenger from God, an answer to prayer.

Why do we use the angel motif at Christmas? The answer must be because the angels announced the birth of Christ to the shepherds. Yet shepherds, although remembered, are not nearly as prominent at Christmas time as the angels. Perhaps the heavenly Father sends forth his messengers year after year to proclaim the anniversary of the birthday of Jesus. Perhaps the weary and indifferent world needs to hear at least once a year that joy does exist, goodwill is offered, and peace on earth is something valuable.

Who are my Christmas angels? Where shall I focus my thoughts and designate individuals as my Christmas angels? The grocery clerk who smiled as she checked my order and asked if I needed assistance is one. I needed that smile and concern as much as I needed the groceries. The former student who sent me a pretty Christmas card and signed it "Your X-student?" The young, friendly neighbor across the road and her four little angels who always wave when they see me. The friends who call and say, "When can we get together?" An anonymous Santa who thrust a candy cane to me and said, "Merry Christmas" as he patted my shoulder. We laughed at each other and I suspect that an angel lived behind the mask.

My dearest Christmas angels are my own two little granddaughters. They make Christmas morning come all the year through. To the small one I say, "Ah, Heather, Heather, what a girl." And she says, "Aw, Grammaw, Grammaw, what a girl." And we laugh together, sharing a special message. To the older one I say, "Goodnight, Angie. God bless you." And she responds in a sleepy voice, "God bless you too, Grammaw." She drifts off to sleep without knowing fear or hunger or hardships and I pray that the angels will always keep her in mind. These are my angels. They came precisely to fulfill my need. I thank God for sending them, visual messages that make life dear.

Christ mentioned that children have guardian angels and as we watch them, we feel a deep gratitude that One who is greater than we has a special mission to guard this child.

At Christmas time we need a host of heavenly angels to sing glad praises, to bring the good message, and to visit each person and bring hope to his heart. We need the awareness that the stranger whose vibrations suddenly make contact with ours, just might be a messenger sent expressly to us from God.

Angels are present throughout the year without fanfare. At Christmas time, we honor them and give them the recognition due them. We try to keep on our best behavior, lest these messengers take a message back to the One who sent them.

Angels sang near Bethlehem
And told the Savior's birth.
They sang a bit of prophecy
That peace would come to earth.

Angels watched the holy child,
And guarded his young life.
God, send out your watchful angels now
And keep each child from strife.

still

The pieces of Christmas lie scattered and bright, strewn across the hearts of many. We look at them collectively and glimpse briefly the twinkling trees, the greens hanging across the cities, the stockings hung, the carols sung, the Yule log lighting dark shadows and warming cold, barren hearts. We see satisfied children and ho-ho-ing Santas and beribboned boxes cached safely away. We see mangers and angels, shepherds and sheep, and soft lights glowing through stained-glass windows splashing rose shadows across the snow.

After the tree is no longer a thing of beauty, after the toys are reality, after the carols have faded from hearing, the pieces of Christmas are carelessly swept from view. They are discarded with pine needles and crushed wrappings and are thought of no longer than the first day of the new year.

Pieces of Christmas remain still. They cannot be, and should not be, discarded after glittering so brightly for only a

Roger Lattner

few short days. A few tenacious shards cling close in sensitive hearts and gleam and glitter all the year through.

Christmas actually means "the mass of Christ." Christmas is the one day those of us who believe in Christ set aside to honor him. If we try to choose one specific time from throughout the year when we feel filled with peace and joy most acutely, most of us would acknowledge that time to be Christmas. Since we are happiest then, we should sprinkle these pieces of Christmas liberally and season each week with rich, Christlike spirit.

Often we see decorative lights strung across porches in April or August and think with smug disapproval that the owners are negligent in leaving Christmas decorations in obvious places when it is no longer the Christmas season. Perhaps our thoughts are accurate, or perhaps the owner wants a visible reminder to practice the habits of Christmas still.

If we act better with a reminder, then let us leave the lights burn all the year long. But the brightest lights are lit in love-filled eyes and are quite exempt from financial cost or the energy crisis. The smiles of Christmas are not out of place even in the drought of August. The merry greetings of friends and the notes of concern and goodwill do not necessarily need to bear the stereotyped motif of Christmas. The messages, however, will serve the same good purpose and bring cheer and attention though the day be bright in June.

Sometimes we read in the newspapers about an unfortunate family whose child suffers a terminal illness. We read that the grieving parents set up a tree and bring gifts to make one more Christmas for the child. Sometimes these activities occur far from December 25th. But Christmas is the manifestation of the most loving and caring time and worth repeating again and again.

In hot July when peaches hang heavy on the trees, it is Christmas still. The orchards are decorated by the hand of God to perfection for our benefit. We view a cherry tree, hanging full of glittering red drops, and know no tree could be decorated nearly as well by a professional decorator. The foliage in autumn is brighter than baubles and in October we can have Christmas still.

It might be a good idea to sing "Silent Night" on a hot night in midsummer and allow the peace and enchantment of God's wondrous love to permeate every cell. The crickets and cicadas and night sounds carol cheerful songs to all who will hear them. We can sing softly in the moonlight in summer and know we have Christmas still.

The magic of Christmas astounds us yearly. When we read in Matthew and Luke the biblical account of the birth of the Baby Jesus, we realize that myriad miracles and God-ordained magic took place.

Much of the same magic has continued throughout the centuries. The Scrooges become kindhearted at Christmas time. The misers buy gifts. The grouch smiles. Life would be magnificent if everyone practiced the traditional feelings all through the year. It would be almost like Christmas morning.

God gave the world an infant to love. Aren't there infants still? The angels sang to the shepherds, men doing their work. Aren't there hard workers still? God placed a star as a beacon to guide wise men to the Christ. Aren't there wise men still?

Roger Lattner

Aren't the heavens still filled with the stars which faithfully give direction and meaning to us on this planet?

Pieces of Christmas lie scattered and broken and beckon and wait for one special season. What a waste of natural resources, hard-earned money, and Herculean effort to limit the effectiveness of Christmas to one specific time.

Even though Christmas is on the opposite side of the calendar, let it be Christmas still. Even when green leaves shimmer and the curled corn stalks reach high in the hot fields, let it be Christmas still. When the children are swimming, their wet bodies gleaming, let it be Christmas still. When school bells ring in September, we can smile and speak kindly to eager young students and let it be Christmas still.

Pieces of Christmas are sweet to the taste. They might make mankind more stable if they were habitually included in his emotional diet.

Pieces of Christmas need to be placed joyfully together and enjoyed as a lovely whole picture and a good way of living throughout the year.

>No matter what month the calendars say,
>Let it be Christmas still.
>If young lambs play on the first day of May,
>Or the fourth of July arcs fire in the sky,
>Smile a smile of goodwill,
>And let it be Christmas still.

Steuben Glass